D1366972

LET'S PLAY BALL

Legends and Lessons from America's Favorite Pastime

Text by **Al Janssen**   Paintings by **Jim Daly**

HARVEST HOUSE™ PUBLISHERS

EUGENE, OREGON

LET'S PLAY BALL

Text Copyright © 2003 by Al Janssen
Published by Harvest House Publishers
Eugene, Oregon 97402

Library of Congress Cataloging-in-Publication Data

Janssen, Al.
    Let's play ball / Al Janssen.
        p. cm.
    Includes bibliographical references.
    ISBN-13: 978-0-7369-1006-4   ISBN-10: 0-7369-1006-9 (alk. paper)
    1. Baseball—Miscellanea. 2. Baseball in art.   I. Title.
    GV873 .J36 2003
    796.357—dc21
2002010619

Artwork copyright © Jim Daly and may not be reproduced without permission.
For more information about art prints featured in this book, please contact:
        Jim Daly
        P.O. Box 25146
        Eugene, OR 97402
        email: caroledaly@earthlink.net

Design and production by Koechel Peterson & Associates, Inc., Minneapolis, Minnesota

Harvest House Publishers and the author have made every effort to trace the ownership of all quotes.
In the event of a question arising from the use of a quote, we regret any error made and will be pleased
to make the necessary correction in future editions of this book.

Printed in China

06 07 08 09 10 11 12 / IM / 10 9 8 7 6 5 4 3

Though the distance between bases has always been a perfect 90 feet, and home plate has remained 17 inches wide, baseball is forever new; a new season, a new game, a new batter. It is constantly surprising, endlessly fascinating, and alternately enrapturing or heart-breaking.

Mark Mulvoy
Managing Editor,
Sports Illustrated

BUILDING MEMORIES

On a late April evening, my son Jonathan and I sat in box seats along the first-base line, about ten rows up from the field, and watched our first game of the season. The Sox and Grizzlies had played seven methodical innings and were knotted in an uninspiring 3–3 tie.

Leading off the bottom of the eighth, our team, the Colorado Springs Sky Sox (the AAA affiliate of the Colorado Rockies), got singles from their first two hitters. As the Fresno Grizzlies pitcher received the ball to pitch to our man Phil Hiatt, I commented to Jonathan, "We get a run or two here, hold them in the ninth, and go home!"

"Sounds good to me!" answered my 16-year-old son.

My teenage boys and I watch a dozen or so major league or AAA games each summer. It's a great way for us to spend a few hours together. Conversation ebbs and flows. Sometimes we're comfortable to sit and watch in silence for several innings. Even on a slow-moving night like this one, we are apt to comment to each other, "I can't think of any other place I'd rather be tonight than at the ballpark!"

The pitcher looked in for his sign, stretched, glanced at second and first, then delivered his pitch. Hiatt swung and rifled a shot toward third base. The third baseman was protecting the line and made a backhanded stab, stepped on third, and threw to second for the double play. The second baseman pivoted over the sliding runner and made a strong relay to first, beating Hiatt by a step.

As the Fresno team jogged off the field, I turned to Jonathan and said, "Did we just see a triple play?"

> *The secret of managing is to keep the guys who hate you away from the guys who are undecided.*
>
> CASEY STENGEL

Jonathan let out a laugh and shook his head. "It happened so fast!"

I wrote "TP 543" in my scorebook, circled the box, and put a big exclamation point next to it.

Neither team scored in the ninth, and our first game of the season headed into extra innings. In the top of the tenth, the Sox shortstop threw wide to first, and the leadoff man was safe. The next batter singled, but then our left fielder made a brilliant running catch for the first out. A strikeout followed, and we were almost out of trouble. On the very next pitch, though, the Grizzlies' catcher crushed the ball over the center-field wall. Now we trailed by three.

> *Baseball is like church.*
> *Many attend.*
> *Few understand.*
>
> LEO DUROCHER

When the first two Sox were retired in the bottom of the inning, I suggested to Jonathan that we start moving toward the exit. As we were walking, our right fielder hit one in the gap to left center and legged out a triple. "Too little, too late," I said, though we sat down near home plate to watch the next hitter walk, which brought up Angel Echevarria. "Well, there's always a chance!" Jonathan countered.

Angel was one of our favorite players. He'd played much of the past two seasons in the Springs, with a couple of quick trips to the show. He stood in the batter's box with a determined look, let one ball pass, then swung furiously at the second

pitch. Jonathan and I stood and stared as the ball soared into the night far over the screen in dead center field. The game was tied again!

By now, most of the original spectators had left for the night. But no way were we leaving! When the crowd had sung "Take Me Out to the Ball Game" three innings earlier, we'd meant it when we'd shouted, "I don't care if I never get back!"

Theoretically, a baseball game can last forever. This one took 12 innings and a shade less than four hours. Phil Hiatt, the man who'd hit into a triple play, became the hero at last by smashing a ball to deep right, where the right fielder hit the wall trying to make a spectacular catch. The force of his collision jarred the ball out of his glove—and the winning run scored on Hiatt's double.

Jonathan and I finally completed the walk to the parking lot that we'd started with two out in the bottom of the tenth. As we passed through the front gate into the night, I couldn't help but remark on this memorable evening. Each team had held the lead three

The Whole Game

Why I have to be at the game for the very first pitch:

I once listened to a game between the Reds and Mets. The leadoff hitter for Cincinnati hit the very first pitch for a home run. The final score was Reds 1, Mets 0.

And why I must also stay for the final out:

Once, on a chilly night as the game was dragging past three hours, my wife complained that she was getting very cold. I took her home and missed a home-team comeback from three runs down—on a grand-slam home run with two outs in the bottom of the ninth.

My conclusion:

How can I enjoy a novel if I skip the first three chapters? How can I solve a mystery if I walk out of a movie with 20 minutes remaining? Likewise, a ball game is a story with a beginning, a middle, and an end. That's why I want to witness the whole drama!

(P.S. I'm sorry I missed that grand slam in the bottom of the ninth, but I don't really mind. After all, my wife's happiness is more important than any game. And now we laugh about how we missed this memory—together!)

Great Moments I Wish I Could Have Seen in Person

Merkle's boner. New York Giants player Fred Merkle failed to touch second on a single that drove in the winning run. The game was declared a tie, and the Giants had to replay the game against the Cubs—and lost it, costing them the pennant in 1908.

A Babe Ruth home run.

A Lou Gehrig home run.

Bobby Thompson's "shot heard round the world" in the 1951 playoff series.

Bill Mazeroski's home run to win the 1960 World Series. It broke my heart, but I still wish I could have been in Forbes Field to see it.

Roger Maris's 61st home run. I'd followed the drama all season, but I missed the final game.

The Miracle Mets of 1969. I watched every pitch of the series, but I wanted to be there at Shea Stadium for the celebration.

Willie Mays making the greatest catch in the '54 Series. Mays was well past his prime when I finally saw him at Dodger Stadium in 1973.

Carlton Fisk's home run in the bottom of the twelfth in Game 6 of the 1975 Series.

Kirk Gibson's one-legged pinch-hit World Series home run that lifted the Dodgers to a game one victory over Oakland.

Cal Ripken Jr.'s 2,131st consecutive game.

times, and there had been four ties. "That's one for the scrapbook!" I exclaimed. I threw my arm around Jonathan's shoulders, and he returned the favor.

"Yeah. That was a great game, Dad!"

It's been more than two years since that evening. There have been thousands of games played in major-league and minor-league parks all over the nation. I wonder if any of the participants even remember this particular night. After all, it was just another game.

But it wasn't just another game for Jonathan and me—it was another memory built together. We've each mentioned it on several occasions since. How can we forget our first triple play? And we'll *never* forget that a game isn't over until—well—until the last out is recorded!

Al Janssen

GOING TO BALL GAMES WITH MY SONS IS A WAY OF CONNECTING, TALKING, AND BUILDING MEMORIES. SURE, NOT EVERY GAME IS AS MEMORABLE AS THE FRESNO–COLORADO SPRINGS CONTEST. BUT THE CUMULATIVE EFFECT OF THOSE COUPLE OF HUNDRED GAMES WE'VE WATCHED TOGETHER IS A BONDING I WOULDN'T TRADE FOR ANYTHING.

BOYHOOD DREAMS

It was late at night and I couldn't sleep.

…*Adrenaline surged as I crouched in center field, my hands barely touching my knees, my body rocking lightly on the balls of my feet.*

Top of the ninth. Game tied. Bases loaded. Two outs.

I peered past the pitcher. The batter, a right-hander, dug in. The shortstop signaled that the next pitch would be off-speed. I leaned to the right. The pitcher stretched to hold the runners close, then delivered. I was already running before I heard the crack of the bat. For an instant I heard the crowd's roar, but as my eyes fastened themselves on the ball I felt myself enter a bubble of silence. I raced towards the left center-field wall.

Just me and the ball. Running faster than I'd ever run. My spikes bit into the warning track and I put my right arm up. I drove my right foot into the padding and leveraged myself as high as I could

> *You gotta be a man to play baseball for a living. But you gotta have a lot of little boy in you.*
>
> ROY CAMPANELLA

go. My right hand grabbed the top of the fence and I pushed still higher as my left hand reached way over my head. My waist fell onto the fence top as I watched the ball land safely in the webbing of my glove. I balanced for a moment on the edge of the fence, then gently fell back to earth.

The crowd's roar filled my ears. I smiled as I juggled the ball lightly in the glove and jogged toward the dugout. Once again Al Janssen had saved the game! And I was batting leadoff in the bottom of the ninth!…

Why am I, a 50-year-old writer, still dreaming of roaming center field in Yankee Stadium long after my athletic career—if I'd had such a career—would be over? What is the power that this game called baseball holds over me?

As a kid I could play an entire baseball game with just a ball and glove and the side of an apartment building in New York City.

A Few of My Favorite Movies

● *The Natural*. What kid hasn't dreamed of having the talent of Roy Hobbs?

● *Field of Dreams*. Based on *Shoeless Joe*, it actually captures the spirit of the book. I tear up when Ray finally gets to play catch with his dad.

● *It Happens Every Spring*. It's a black-and-white picture from 1949. A college professor discovers a liquid that repels wood, and he uses it on baseballs to become a pitcher in the majors.

● *The Rookie*. Based on a true story, Jim Morris fulfills the dream of many a middle-aged man by rising from high-school teacher to major-league pitcher over the course of a single season.

● On a sadder note: The movie *Eight Men Out* is an authentic depiction of the Black Sox scandal of 1919.

● Finally, everyone should watch a few hours of Ken Burns's masterpiece documentary, *Baseball*.

I would toss the ball in the air and make running catches. I'd pitch against the brick wall and run to field grounders. Mentally I did play-by-play: "Tony Kubek backhands the ball in the hole, fires to Bobby Richardson at second. Richardson jumps over the runner and relays to first. In time! Double play!! The Yankees win again!"

One spring I acquired a rubber baseball that was guaranteed to curve. But I was more interested in hitting it, because there was a sweet spot on one side, and when I connected just right, the ball flew farther than I'd ever hit a ball before.

One day as a friend tossed pitches to "Mickey Mantle"—me—I pounded grounders and weak pop-ups...until the one perfect swing against the sweet spot. The ball soared up and up, arced gracefully, and disappeared onto the roof of the building across the street. Though I never saw the ball again, I didn't grieve its loss. My "pitcher" gaped, his mouth open at the blast. The apartments around me were now a stadium filled with yelling, awe-struck fans. For one glorious moment I felt what Mickey Mantle experienced 40 or 50 times a season when he sent a baseball soaring into the bleachers.

In winter the games moved indoors. My friends and I would wad up paper balls, grab a slim textbook, and play home-run derby in an empty classroom. Occasionally we'd acquire a ball of aluminum foil, and then we could play several nine-inning games without it unraveling like the paper wads did.

As an adult, my fantasies subsided, until they were revived by my sons. As I started playing catch with them in the backyard, I imagined one or both of them growing up to play in the big leagues. I prayed that they hadn't inherited my lack of athletic skill. My five-foot-nine frame yielded little power as a hitter. I couldn't run fast, and never threw that hard. But a deep sense of satisfaction emerged just through tossing a ball with my boys, then setting them up with a fat, red plastic bat and trying to groove pitches to their natural swing so they could experience the joy of hitting.

One evening, I arrived home from work dog-tired. I went to the backyard to toss pitches to my six-year-old son. He had struggled to hit with any consistency the pitches I'd grooved to him. Then in one magical moment, he swung perfectly with a slight uppercut and sent the Wiffle ball soaring over the roof of our house and into the front yard! The joy on his face was also my joy. I ran through

the living room to retrieve the ball, shouting to Jo and our guests, "Josh just hit his first home run!" Certainly he was now on his way to major-league stardom. My retirement was secure!

Unfortunately, as my boys graduated to hardballs and metal bats, I learned the sad truth. Their basic athletic abilities were no better than mine. Jonathan was willing to try for a while, and I worked out with him at a nearby field, hitting practice grounders and flies and pitching batting practice.

One spring morning, Jon took his cuts. I grooved a few pitches, and he lined some singles into the outfield. I picked up a fresh ball, one I'd acquired at a minor-league game a few years back. I juggled it a couple of times in my hand, suddenly feeling the old, familiar surge of adrenaline. This was the mound of dreams. I was a big-league pitcher facing a dangerous hitter. The count was three

All the ballparks and the big crowds have a certain mystique. You feel attached, permanently wedded to the sounds that ring out, to the fans chanting your name, even when there are only four or five thousand in the stands on a Wednesday afternoon.

MICKEY MANTLE

balls, two strikes. I had to get this out. I leaned forward to catch my sign, nodded at the imaginary catcher, and gripped the ball with my index finger along the inside of the stitches.

I rocked back on the rubber, raised my arms overhead, then threw, snapping my wrist as the ball rolled off my fingers—"like pulling down a window shade," as one of my coaches long ago had taught me. The ball flew toward Jon. His eyes widened. But before it struck him, it broke and dipped across the heart of the plate. A perfect curve! "Steeeriiike three!" I shouted as I pumped my fist.

Jon stared at me, then exclaimed, "Dad, what was that?"

"Son, *that* was a curveball!"

Jonathan grinned and shook his head. The crowd cheered. I removed my cap to acknowledge their accolades. For a moment, I was a kid again!

A Night to Remember

"Anna, how about we go to a ball game?"

"Okay, Daddy!" my daughter answered.

Unlike my sons, Anna wasn't always willing to spend a night at the ballpark with her father. There were dolls to dress, books to read, friends to talk with—or she could spend hours practicing volleyball serves against the side of our house.

Until one magical evening in Kansas City. We were on the first night of a three-week vacation to Williamsburg and Washington, D.C. The boys and I wanted to collect another major-league stadium along the way. Royals Stadium was Mom and Anna's concession to that desire.

It was "Roll Back the Prices" night. So we gathered $1 hot dogs and drinks and sat in the third deck, right behind home plate. Ten minutes before the first pitch, the ground crew charged the field and covered it with the tarp. The public-address announcer warned us to take cover against an approaching storm. We were moving higher, up under the roof, when we heard the crash of thunder.

For the next hour, rain lashed the stadium in sheets, and lightning and thunder put on a show as good as any fireworks. Anna leaned against me and grinned. "Daddy, this is fun!"

With the storm finally passed, the ground crew prepared the field, and the game began. Now the fireworks came from the batter's box. The Angels were leading the home team 4–1 in the bottom of the sixth, when the Royals launched four home runs. Never before had Kansas City hit four homers in a single inning. Anna jumped up and cheered them all.

As the Royals completed their 9–4 win, the pyrotechnics started. For another 20 minutes we enjoyed the best fireworks show we'd ever seen before we headed back to our hotel.

Not bad for my daughter's first big league game.

But now, when we head to the ballpark together, I feel compelled to remind her, "Anna, not every game you see will be that exciting."

And her reply always sets off a few little fireworks in my heart. "That's all right, Daddy. Whatever happens, it will be fun just being with you."

THE RADIO

Beginning in early March with spring-training games and continuing through the summer months, my radio is often tuned to a ball game. I listen to play-by-play while working in the garage, firing up the barbecue, taking a shower, or running errands around town.

My love of baseball was born at the mikes of Mel Allen, Phil Rizzuto, and Red Barber, who created the verbal pictures that brought the New York Yankees to life. In summer New York City vibrated to the sounds of baseball. You could hear the game on tenement steps, in taxicabs, at newsstands, or from the portable radio of the doorman at a downtown skyscraper. Ask for the score and you'd get a cryptic, "Yanks lead 1–0, bottom of the third."

Radio was a vital link during the World Series, which until 1971 was always played in the afternoons. For weekday games, my buddies and I would sneak a radio into class. Sometimes if we were discovered, the teacher would frown and tell us, "I'll hold that for you until the end of the period." More often, he'd ignore the violation but want to know the score as the bell sounded for us to move to the next class.

During hot summers, my favorite weekend activity began when my father would give me two quarters. I would ride 21 stories down the elevator, buy a hot dog—sans sauerkraut—and a soda from the street-corner vendor, then sit on a park bench outside my apartment building and turn on the radio. "Hello, everybody!" Mel Allen would open in his distinctive nasal twang. Later Red Barber would lend his more gentlemanly southern voice, and Phil would add his boyish enthusiasm, exclaiming "Holy Cow!" after some great play on the field.

> *It could be.*
> *It might be.*
> *It is!*
> *A home run!*
>
> Play-by-play broadcaster
> HARRY CARAY'S
> home-run call

The only thing better than listening to one game was absorbing a Sunday doubleheader. All afternoon I could soak up the sun and revel in the drama, ignoring for a few hours that I had no friends in the apartment complex and hated living in the big city.

We lived on 124th Street in Manhattan, between Amsterdam and Broadway. From the top floor of my family's co-op apartment I could see Yankee Stadium in the Bronx. Though it was just a short subway ride away, I attended only two or three games there as a boy, all with schoolmates. So my only link to the great stadium, with its bright lights calling to me at night as though it were the Promised Land, was via the radio. When Mickey Mantle or Roger Maris batted, I assumed my latest "lucky position," hoping to hear the loud crack of the bat, the rising roar of the crowd, and Mel Allen cheering, "It's going, going, gone!"

In 1962, another team was added to the New York baseball world, the expansion New York Mets, who played their first two seasons in the ancient Polo Grounds. Their broadcast team was headed by Lindsey Nelson, who was supported by Bob Murphy and former home-run slugger Ralph Kiner. The team they described was the opposite of the powerful Yanks across the river. In their first season, the Mets set a standard for futility, losing their first 9 games, and soon thereafter lost another 17 straight. Hearing the announcer describe a routine pop-up was cause for great alarm: "This should be an easy play. Ohhh no, Throneberry drops the ball!" Marv Throneberry and the Mets wound up the year with 120 losses, a record that's stood for more than 40 years.

But like a kid chasing screaming fire engines to a three-alarm blaze, I followed the Mets and found myself rooting passionately for them. On June 20, 1963, the Yankees and Mets met in the Mayor's Trophy Game for the benefit of sandlot baseball in the city. It may have been a meaningless exhibition, but to Mets fans, this was our World Series. I listened to the game in bed, with the radio under my pillow so as not to disturb my sister, and quietly cheered as the Mets' regulars defeated the Yankee scrubs 6–2.

Following a late-night ball game in bed was another of my common summer activities. Many a night I fell asleep listening to a broadcast through an earpiece—and was awakened at two or three in the morning by strange voices or the crash of my transistor radio falling to the floor.

The magic of radio was in how it stimulated my imagination. I couldn't attend the games, but I could be there in my mind. It was better than television with its black-and-white picture and limited views. With radio I could "see" the whole field as the announcer drew a picture. It was a lush stage on which marvelous dramas played themselves out—stories that shaped my life. They showed me that the best teams still lose 50 or 60 or 70 games in a season, that the worst teams can win on any given day, and that even the twenty-fifth man on the roster can be an unexpected hero.

It's amazing to recall some of those dramas years later. One sultry Friday night in August 1963, I tuned in to follow the Mets versus the Cubs at the Polo Grounds. I had taken to following a lanky right-handed pitcher named Roger Craig. He'd led the Mets' staff the first season by winning 10 games against 24 losses. He actually pitched better in the second season, defeating the great Sandy Koufax for his second victory. Then his luck ran out. Loss mounted upon loss. Five times he allowed the opposition only one run, yet he lost all five decisions by 1–0 scores. By early August, Roger's record was 2 wins and 20

> *Little League baseball is a good thing 'cause it keeps the parents off the streets and the kids out of the house.*
>
> YOGI BERRA

Great Memories

Here are a few priceless memories of games I've attended with my sons:

Our first time to see the Rockies. My sons and I baked in the sun as we sat in the left-field bleachers at Mile High Stadium during Colorado's inaugural season. We arrived two hours early for batting practice. And we stayed through the very last pitch. Even though Philadelphia beat our Rockies 18–1, we had a blast, and we've reminisced many times about that Sunday.

Wrigley Field. A Thursday afternoon. Cardinals versus Cubs. Jonathan and I had tickets on the lower level, even with third base. "Watch Ozzie Smith," I coached my son. "The Cardinals shortstop is the best ever." That day the future Hall of Famer had the best offensive day of his career—five hits, six runs batted in.

A winner-take-all final game for the Pacific Coast League Championship. Joshua and I watched our Sky Sox battle Salt Lake. The Buzz led 5–1, but Colorado Springs battled back. Down a run in the bottom of the ninth, they scored twice to take the championship. We stayed for 45 minutes afterward to savor it with the players as they celebrated on the field.

losses, and his 18 straight "L's" tied the National League record. I had to follow this story to see if his luck could change.

In the first four innings, Roger shut out the Cubs, and Frank Thomas homered to give New York a lead. After saying my prayers and turning out the light, I continued to listen to the game in the dark, gazing out my apartment window at the Hudson River and the New Jersey shore. Both teams scored twice in the fifth. In the top of the eighth, the Cubs' Billy Williams tripled, and Ron Santo drove him home with a fly ball. So the game was tied going into the bottom of the ninth.

By now, I had tried every lucky position, hoping against logic that I might somehow influence the outcome. If the Mets got a hit while I was lying on my back, I remained rigid until the runner died on base. If Roger gave up a hit, I crossed my fingers and held my breath until he struck out a batter to escape the threat. This gallant pitcher pitched all nine innings, striking out eight, walking one, and giving up eight hits. Now he needed one run to earn the victory.

I'm sure I must have prayed as I listened. I desperately wanted Roger's effort to be rewarded.

By my moral reasoning, why should he go into the record books for futility when he'd pitched so well? It was one thing to get shelled night after night. It was quite another to pitch your heart out and lose.

The leadoff hitter flied out. There followed a single, and I pumped my fist, saying nothing so as not to disturb my sister. But she was awake. "Are they going to win?" she whispered.

It didn't look promising when Choo Choo Coleman struck out. Then Al Moran drove a double down the left-field line, and the roar of 11,000 fans filled my earpiece. Lindy McDaniel relieved the Cubs starter, and manager Casey Stengel sent up a pinch hitter for Craig, who was promptly walked intentionally.

The tension was unbearable. I sat up in bed as Jim Hickman came up to hit. Lindsey Nelson, I recall, breathlessly called, *Strike. Ball. Another strike. Another ball.* Then the count went to three and two. "The runners will all be running on the pitch," the voice on the radio said. "And here it comes.

> *It's a beautiful day.*
> *Let's play two!*
>
> ERNIE BANKS

"Hickman hits a fly ball to left. Williams backs up against the wall. He should catch it…" And I instantly thought, *At least Roger didn't lose.*

Then I heard, "It's a grand-slam home run! I don't believe it! The ball hit the scoreboard. The Mets win. The players are charging the field to celebrate. Unbelievable!!"

I couldn't restrain a muted shout of joy. In my imagination, I *saw* the scene. The upper deck hung over the field. The left fielder had caught the ball, but since the ball had barely nicked the stands, it was a home run!

Today, I no longer hide my radio under a pillow, but radio broadcasts still feed my love for baseball. As I hear the announcer's description, I am sitting in the press box, right behind home plate. I see the entire field, the positioning of each player, the third-base coach flashing his signs, the runner leading off as the pitcher goes into his stretch.

Then comes that familiar surge of adrenaline. I hear the crack of the bat, and no matter what I'm doing, I can't help but lean forward slightly to catch the flight of the ball.

KEEPING SCORE

"Dad, why do you keep score?"

One of my boys asked me that question as we settled into our seats at Coors Field on a warm June evening. Tonight, we were in row two of the third deck in right field, giving us a panoramic view of the Rocky Mountains. With one son on either side, I opened my scorebook and started filling in the starting lineups: "Pittsburgh Pirates: Martin, 8; Bell, 6…; Colorado Rockies:…"

"Boys, I've been keeping score for more than 30 years. It's my way of enjoying the game. It keeps me involved as I track the unfolding drama on the field."

When I was first listening to Yankee broadcasts, Red Barber or Mel Allen would casually mention something like "That's 6 to 4 if you're scoring." I always wondered what that meant— until that wondrous day at summer camp when Trinity played a ball game against Camp Mohawk.

I wasn't in the starting lineup, and the coach asked me, "Will you keep the scorebook?"

I didn't know how to keep score, but two innings later, I was in the game and collected two hits. After the game, I looked at the scoresheet and saw my name, with a record of two singles and one run scored. Somehow, those accomplishments, permanently recorded for future historians, felt more real.

That scorebook came home with me after camp. I don't know how I learned the numbers associated with each position: "1" for pitcher, "2" for catcher, "3" for first base, and so on. But on August 29, 1962, I kept score of a doubleheader between the Cleveland Indians and the New York Yankees.

From then on, I was hooked. That evening at Coors Field, I was working on my eighteenth scorebook, and I'd previously recorded more than

> *Ninety feet between the bases is the nearest thing to perfection that man has yet achieved.*
>
> RED SMITH
> Sportswriter

400 amateur and minor- and major-league games. (There were many more scoresheets that, sadly, were gone—tossed in a moment of insanity. I'd collected them during the '70s, when I had regularly attended major-league games on a press pass and used the scorecards provided in the press box.)

Now my sons and I were going to watch the Rockies and the Pirates. "Three hours from now, one team will likely have won." I threw my arms around my sons as I talked. "But which one? And who will be the star? Will we see a pitching duel or a slugging match? And what will be the critical moment that decides the game? It could happen on the first pitch. It could happen in the fourth or fifth inning. Or it might come down to the final play of the game! You never know. But whatever happens, we'll be able to recall the details years from now—because I kept score."

As I finished my point, I wrote "With Joshua and Jonathan" at the top of a page. That was a habit I'd started in recent years. Now each game had added meaning because I knew the memory was shared with a family member or friend.

We stood for the national anthem, then settled down for the first pitch—a ball, fired by Marvin Freeman to the Pirates' center fielder, Martin. I wrote "1" in the tiny boxes used to keep track of balls and strikes. On a 2–0 pitch, Martin grounded to second. Jason Bates fielded it and threw to Andres Galarraga for out number one. "He was fortunate to get the out on a 2–0 count," I remarked. We regularly passed such comments among the three of us throughout the game.

A Few of My Favorite Books

Of any sport, baseball has produced the finest writing. I have a shelf full of my favorites. Sometimes, on a cold winter night, I pull down a volume and dream of sunny afternoons at the ballpark.

Here are a few I enjoy reading again and again:

NONFICTION

- *A Day in the Bleachers* by Arnold Hano. The author puts you in a famous World Series game. In your mind, you see Willie Mays running straight toward you, making the greatest catch in history.
- Any book by Roger Angell. I've read *The Summer Game* so many times that it's now bound together by a rubber band.
- *The Boys of Summer* by Roger Kahn. He makes me wish I could have watched the Dodgers play in Ebbets Field.

FICTION

- *The Celebrant* by Eric Rolfe Greenberg. It's about baseball during the first two decades of the twentieth century, and the great Christy Mathewson.
- *Shoeless Joe* by W.P. Kinsella. "If you build it, he will come." The magic occurs in an Iowa cornfield.
- *If I Never Get Back* by Darryl Brock. On the way home from his father's funeral, an angry man steps off the train and finds himself barnstorming with the Cincinnati Reds of 1869.

AND JUST FOR FUN!

- Everyone should read "The Curious Case of Sidd Finch" by George Plimpton. It was originally published as an April Fools joke by *Sports Illustrated* in 1985. I fell for it! You can find it in anthologies. I keep rereading it because I wish it were true.
- If you can't decide what to read, then check out a copy of *The Fireside Book of Baseball* and open up to any place in the book.

There was no score after the first inning. "Freeman threw 20 pitches, Loaiza only 12," I observed. The boys knew what that meant. By keeping score, we could follow the effectiveness of each pitcher, see who was working harder and might tire, observe who was getting ahead of the hitters and who might be struggling with control.

The game moved along nicely. Colorado took the first lead in the second, but Pittsburgh led 2–1 after five. Between innings I flipped back through the pages of my current scorebook. "This first page was a game I saw last year with my good friend Sealy Yates." The scoresheet the boys saw on my lap revealed that the Angels had defeated the White Sox 3–2. Three days later my sons and I had attended our last game at Mile High Stadium to watch the Braves play the Rockies. "We were in the south stands," Joshua remarked. "And Andres Galarraga hit that tremendous home run."

"That's right. A three-run shot in the sixth."

Josh looked at the page. "But the Braves still won."

> *The Giants win the pennant!*
> *The Giants win the pennant!*
> *The Giants win the pennant!*
>
> RUSS HODGE's home-run call when Bobby Thompson hit "the shot heard round the world" to win the 1951 Playoffs

We flipped several pages. "This game we saw as a family with the Johnsons," Jon noted for June 18. The Johnsons were our neighbors across the street, and we'd enjoyed a tailgate picnic in the parking lot before the game.

The next day was Father's Day. "I remember that—the Sox won the first-half championship," Joshua noted.

"That was a great comeback!" Jon added.

We continued to relive memories between the innings of the game in front of us. July 4: The whole family had attended and enjoyed fireworks during the game—a 10–9 win for the home team—plus a great fireworks show after the final out.

"Here's a playoff game, Dad," Jon observed. "Why didn't you take me?"

I laughed. "It was a school night. I'm sorry." I'd attended that game with three friends, and Chris Jones had hit three home runs, including the game winner in the bottom of the tenth.

The game in front of us had now reached the ninth inning. The Rockies' closer was pitching, but he couldn't hold the 4–3 lead. Martin, the leadoff hitter, tied it with a home run. So we moved to the bottom of the ninth. No longer were we reminiscing; we were engrossed in the drama. Joe Girardi singled to left. Walt Weiss sacrificed him to second. A left-handed hitter was announced. The Pirates countered with a left-handed pitcher. The Rockies immediately pinch-hit for the pinch hitter. But the left-handed pitcher walked that batter intentionally to set up a lefty–lefty matchup. But Rockies manager Don Baylor countered with a right-handed pinch hitter, Ellis Burks. Pittsburgh brought in right-handed pitcher Dan Miceli.

The boys and I analyzed each of these moves and decided that Baylor had his best pinch hitter up with a chance to win the game, and that Pittsburgh had countered with a tough right-handed pitcher. So who had chosen right? Who had miscalculated?

Miceli threw ball one. Then ball two. Burks fouled off a pitch to the screen behind him— "He had it timed well," I noted.

"Yeah," Jon added, "the pitcher needs to change speed. Burks loves fast balls."

Miceli leaned in for his sign, then checked the runners. The three of us leaned forward. The pitcher threw. Burks swung, and the ball rose on a line toward center field. The three of us jumped up as the center fielder raced back to the fence. But he ran out of room. We raised our arms as the ball landed in front of the fountains just below us, to our right. Looking back toward the infield, we watched the three runners triumphantly tour the bases while Miceli slowly walked from the mound to the visitors' dugout.

It's been six-and-a-half years since Colorado beat Pittsburgh 7–4 on that balmy June night. But for my sons and me, those memories come back to life—all of the moves by the managers matching wits, all the unfolding of the drama, until Ellis Burks with one swing of the bat announces, "Checkmate!"

And thanks to that little scorebook, ten years from now, if we want, we can savor that night again.

REFLECTIONS ON A HERO

We were driving home from a vacation in Oregon when the news came over the car radio: "Baseball legend Mickey Mantle is dead from liver cancer at the age of 63…"

Without warning I felt the tears start to flow. "Are you okay?" my wife asked. From the back of the minivan, my daughter shouted, "Why is Daddy crying?"

Why was Daddy crying over the death of a baseball player? Why did so many other men, as I later learned, cry over this news? Is it possible that somehow, someway, a part of our youth died with that legend?

As I struggled to control my emotions, I started talking to my carful of captive listeners. "I remember, as a kid, watching him play in Yankee Stadium." I glanced in the rearview mirror at my sons. They were listening.

> *A team is where a boy can prove his courage on his own. A gang is where a coward goes to hide.*
>
> MICKEY MANTLE

"I attended my first game there about 1956, when I was in first or second grade. We were high up in the stands, and I didn't understand the game. But when Mantle came up to bat, there was an excitement in the crowd, and one of my classmates told me to clap my hands as we chanted, 'We want a hit! We want a hit!' Then a cheer erupted as the faraway figure lined a single into right field. That's the only memory I have of my first major-league game.

"A few years later, I attended another Yankees game with my sixth-grade class. It was against the Baltimore Orioles, and at some point they put Hoyt Wilhelm in as pitcher. The catcher changed to this oversized mitt to catch Wilhelm's knuckleball. They don't allow such large mitts today."

I glanced again at my sons. They weren't bothered by narrative detour. "Mantle was the star that day. I can still see him hitting a line drive that landed in the right-field bull pen for the decisive run."

From that point on, Mickey Mantle was my hero. He was greater than Superman. He could run, field, and hit, and it seemed like he was the decisive factor in many games. In 1961, I rooted for him to win the home-run race against teammate Roger Maris and break the most famous record in sports—Babe Ruth's 60 home runs in one season. I had no animus against Maris—but Mantle was special, almost godlike to this impressionable boy.

> *Baseball is caring. Player and fan alike must care, or there is no game.*
>
> WILLIAM SAROYAN
> *Sports Illustrated*

"Mantle was a switch-hitter, and he could hit long home runs from either side of the plate," I told my family. "In the '64 series against the Cardinals, he came up in the bottom of the ninth of a tie game and blasted a monster home run to win the game. That home run broke Babe Ruth's record of 15 homers in World Series competition."

I was babbling. What was the point? Sure, Mantle was a great athlete. But there was something more, something deeper I needed to probe. I recalled how in 1964 I was given a book called *The Quality of Courage: True Stories of Heroism and Bravery,* written by Mickey Mantle. I still remember the impression it made on me. Though it contained stories of baseball players performing despite injuries and pain, it was the daily courageous actions of ordinary men that impressed me even more.

One story was about a group of men gathered in a cabin after a day of skiing. They were using oil lamps since there was no electricity. Such lamps were dangerous if tipped over or dropped—they could make a wooden structure go up in flames instantly. One of the men absentmindedly picked up a lamp that was sitting by the chimney. Though it was scorching his hand, if he dropped it, the cabin would certainly ignite. But he didn't let it fall. Calmly he set it down despite the pain. "Boy, that hurts!" he exclaimed, his hand a mass of blisters. "How come you didn't drop that lamp?" his friend asked in amazement. The man was surprised by the question. "Drop it? It would have set the place on fire."

It's strange how certain stories impact a young man. Why that particular one? Perhaps because it showed me that real men do what is right whatever the cost. That was part of the Mantle mystique. He had severely injured his knee in the 1951 World Series and thereafter always played in pain. He was my athletic god—but with the "Achilles' heel" of persistent injuries, which brought him back down to earth.

Get Your Hot Dogs!

I don't remember who won the first game I saw at Yankee Stadium, but I do remember ordering a hot dog from the vendor roaming the stands. I was only seven years old and remained mute as I reluctantly passed the money down to the aisle. The vendor ceremoniously took out a bun, placed the dog in it reverently, and then—to my horror—slathered mustard over the sausage and passed the whole thing back down the row.

Carefully, with my index finger, I wiped off the yellow mixture. But I had no napkin! What was a boy to do? I looked right, then left, then straight ahead at the green jacket of the man in front of me. Very gently, so he wouldn't feel it, I wiped my finger on that green jacket. More than 40 years have passed now, and many times I've wondered what that man's wife said to him when he returned home from the game and she observed the yellow mess on his back.

As I grew older and learned more about the great Mick, I discovered another side, a far less heroic portrait. "Mantle was far from perfect," I said to my boys. "He didn't take care of himself as a ballplayer. As great as he was, he could have been so much greater. What if he'd really worked out and taken care of his body? He hit 536 home runs in his career. Maybe he could have hit 200 more. I think he could have been the greatest that ever played."

Could have been. What sad words those are. I had been shocked when I saw Mantle one time at an old-timers' celebration in Portland. He and another baseball great were joking around, ignoring the fans. They appeared to be drunk. "He was a flawed human being," I said. Then, after a pause,

I added, "But aren't we all." How poignant the words Mantle had uttered near the end of his life: "Don't be like me. I'm no role model!"

I read all of the news accounts of the Mick after his death. At his funeral, which was attended by many baseball greats, the eulogy was delivered by TV announcer Bob Costas. But it was the words of Bobby Richardson, second baseman for the Yankees when I was a boy, that particularly caught my attention. Richardson told how he'd gone to Mantle's hospital bed in the final week of his life and said, "Mickey, I love you, and I want you to spend eternity in heaven with me."

According to Richardson, the Mick asked for and received the forgiveness he so desperately needed. "How great to know that in the ninth inning of his life, with two outs and two strikes, Mickey Mantle hit an eternal home run on his last pitch."

> Bravery is a complicated thing to describe. You can't say it's three feet long and two feet wide and that it weighs four hundred pounds or that it's colored bright blue or that it sounds like a piano or that it smells like roses. It's a quality, not a thing.
>
> MICKEY MANTLE
> *The Quality of Courage*

Somehow Mantle's journey reflected the yearnings of a baby boomer like me:

The desire to be a great ballplayer.

The frustration of not fulfilling our full potential.

The failure to live up to the hero image of so many kids.

The hope that, in the end, and despite all of our failings, redemption is offered.

Yes, I think that was it. That was the "something deeper." Mickey Mantle's story was, in a way, my story. I never played big-league ball, but I understood the frustration of my human limitations. And I'd also discovered the redeeming love of God.

"Boys," I concluded, "learn the lesson of Mickey Mantle. Don't make the mistakes he made. And most of all, you don't have to wait till the end of your life to learn that God's love is there for you right now."

RAIN DELAY

On his fifteenth birthday, Jonathan found a birthday card on the breakfast table. I had already left for work, but I couldn't help visualizing his expression as he opened the card and read these words:

"Ken Griffey Jr. requests your presence tonight at his game between the Seattle Mariners and the Colorado Rockies at Coors Field. He promises to hit a home run for you if you bring your dad." Enclosed were two tickets.

I was glad we had seats on the mezzanine level under the roof, for I could see the clouds building over the Front Range as we drove to Denver from Colorado Springs. The game was scheduled to begin at 5:35, but a shower delayed the first pitch by 45 minutes. So we ate some grilled hot dogs and waited patiently.

When the contest finally started, our eyes focused on the athlete roaming center field for

> *Baseball, more than any other, is a generational game. It speaks best across the years.*
>
> FRANK DEFORD
> *Sports Illustrated*

the Mariners. Ken Griffey had been Jon's favorite player for several years, but he had never seen him in play in person. Only with the advent of interleague play had the possibility arisen that Griffey's American League team would visit the Rockies.

The M's scored twice in the first. The Rockies answered with a home run by Angel Echevarria, one of the players we had enjoyed watching when he was with the Sky Sox, the Rockies' AAA team that played just a couple of miles from our home. In the third, Edgard Clemente came up to bat. He was another talented player from our AAA team, one who'd just been called up to the show. On the second pitch, he launched a shot over the center-field fence for his first major-league home run. That hit ignited the Rockies, and they scored five more times to take a 7–2 lead.

Strange Plays I Wish I'd Seen

Babe Herman doubles into a double play. In 1926, Brooklyn's Babe Herman hit a bases-loaded double against Boston. However, initially the runner at second held up, thinking the ball might be caught. The runner at first dashed to third, and Babe was certain his hit was a triple, so he also ran to third. Three runners wound up standing on third base. The Boston third baseman tagged them all, and two were called out.

The 24-inch home run. It happened in a minor-league game between Minneapolis and St. Paul in the early 1900s. It had rained hard the previous day, and the grounds were extremely soggy. Shortstop Andy Oyler came to bat and ducked away from a pitch at his head. Everyone heard a loud crack. Had the ball hit Oyler? He was running madly around the bases as the fielders looked up for the ball. Only after Oyler crossed home was the mystery solved. The ball had struck the bat as Oyler ducked—and it had landed in the mud just two feet in front of home plate!

The player who went one-for-three in a single at-bat. Jeffrey Leonard pinch-hit for Houston in the bottom of the ninth against the New York Mets. He lifted a fly ball to center field for the final out of the game. However, time had been called before the pitch, so Leonard hit again and this time lined a single to left. But during the time-out, the Met first baseman had gone to the dugout. The game couldn't officially resume without nine fielders. And so Leonard was told to bat a third time. This time he flied out to truly end the game.

It was raining again as Griffey came up to bat to lead off the fourth. We leaned forward to watch the left-handed pitcher battle the left-handed hitter. Griffey was quickly down two strikes, but fouled off one pitch and took three balls. Then he swung. A crack reverberated through the stadium as the ball shot upward. We leaped up, knowing instantly that it was gone. The ball appeared to be still rising as it slammed against the façade of the third deck in right field and then fell back to the field.

Jonathan and I stood slack-jawed. The ball had left the yard so fast that we could scarcely imagine the power with which it had been hit. The message board in left field announced the distance: "476 feet!"

It was one of those crazy games in which neither team can ever score enough runs. Colorado was holding an 11–7 lead in the seventh when Griffey made his fourth appearance at the plate, with runners at first and third. This time he lined a shot over the center fielder's head. Again we stood in awe as the superstar sped around the bases, sliding into third base. A moment later he scored on a ground ball to short, and the Mariners were only a single run behind.

But then the heavens opened up and the rain poured in earnest. The field was cleared, and the tarp was rolled over the infield.

Baseball is unique among games in that it is at the mercy of the elements. Football can be played in a steady downpour or in freezing conditions. Basketball and hockey are played indoors. But baseball must endure the elements. When the rain comes, the game must wait. And what do fans do during a rain delay? They talk.

"Haven't we been here before?" I asked Jon as we propped up our feet on the seats in front of us.

"My thirteenth birthday!" he reminded me. "Braves and Rockies. They stopped it in the second inning. We waited two-and-a-half hours."

"That's right!" I laughed. "And you refused to go home. That was your birthday present, and you were going to see the game to its conclusion."

> *I think I'll have more value at anything I do later on for having been a baseball player.*
>
> JIM BOUTON
> *Ball Four*

"I'm glad we did. It was a good game! The Rockies beat Tom Glavine."

"And we got home at 2:30 in the morning. I got only three hours of sleep before I had to get up and go to work."

The spray from the downpour was starting to hit us, so we rose and went inside to continue our talk. We strolled along the concourse, watching through the windows as the rain fell across the powerful lights of Coors Field. The water on the tarp twinkled under the constant pounding of the raindrops.

"Remember the Sunday game we attended where the weather changed just as the game started?" I asked. Jonathan looked up at me in expectation. "One of the Sky Sox players hit a routine foul ball…"

"Yeah!" he chimed in. "The wind blew it fair, and it landed next to third base for a double."

"That game lasted one inning before it was called."

It was Jonathan who recalled the greatest rainstorm of all: "This can't compare to *that* night." The game had begun on a clear, warm summer night. For five innings we enjoyed a pitching duel while watching a lightning show beyond left field. Thundershowers often circle the stadium, and we never know whether they will miss us or interrupt the game. But this storm descended, and we raced up the steps to shelter.

We soon realized that this was no ordinary deluge. Lightning ripped through the sky every few seconds, and thunder followed instantly. Perhaps for fear of a direct lightning strike, the lights were turned off. Huddled in the crowd, we gazed out onto the darkened field. Lightning flashed again and again, revealing vast sheets of rain. Within 15 minutes, the water began to rise over the infield. Obviously this game wasn't going to be resumed, but I didn't want to drive until the rain slackened. Jonathan huddled close to me, in awe, as I was, of the power of this storm. We followed the rising of the waters. An hour after the game had stopped, the lightning flashes revealed that the *entire* playing field was under water. Huddled in the concourse, we half expected the stadium to rise and float, making itself into an ark to save the faithful fans.

Finally, we had no choice but to try to

drive home. We waded through four inches of rushing water in the parking lot to where our van was parked. At the first intersection, the lights were out of order, and we saw several abandoned cars. A mile from home there were piles of ice from heavy hail—and for a couple of blocks it looked like winter. When we finally pulled into our driveway, Jo met us at the door and clutched us in an embrace. "I was so worried!" was all she could say.

The next morning, the paper revealed that six inches of rain had fallen in a single hour.

◆　　◆　　◆　　◆

"So this rain delay is nothing!" Jonathan laughed as we made the turn at the end of the Coors Field club level and began to retrace our steps.

We traversed the third deck, then descended to the field level, enjoying the stadium, the lights, the music blaring from the speakers. Two hours—and the rain hadn't let up. Most of the fans had already abandoned the game. "How long do we wait?" I asked.

"Do you think they'll call it?" he asked.

"This is a well-engineered field. It can

Records Are Made to Be Broken

In 1973, I recorded my belief that there were five unbreakable individual records in baseball. In a piece for *Athletes in Action* magazine called "The Untouchables," I listed these records as safe:

- Most hits
- Most consecutive games played
- Most complete games pitched
- Most total bases
- Most consecutive games batted safely

Rather cocky for a 24-year-old sportswriter. Today, I humbly admit that three of those records have been shattered.

- Pete Rose bested Ty Cobb for the most career hits.
- Cal Ripken Jr. bettered Lou Gehrig's record for consecutive games by 500.
- And Hank Aaron shattered Stan Musial's record for total bases.

As for the other two records:

- In this age of relief specialists, I'm "confident" no one is going to pitch 749 complete games as Cy Young did.
- And Joe DiMaggio's record of hitting in 56 consecutive games…well, it's lasted more than 60 years.

handle a lot of rain. Plus, this is the last time the two teams play this season. My guess is that they'll try to finish the game."

The rain let up, and the umpires and managers examined the field. They appeared ready to order the tarp removed, when the mist became another steady downpour. "Son, you know I hate to leave a ball game before it's over. But it's going to be midnight before they start again, and we have a long drive back…"

"And you have to go to work tomorrow. I know, Dad. It's okay—really!"

◆　◆　◆　◆

We drove home in the rain, and as we neared Colorado Springs, the game resumed. We listened to the broadcast of the final two innings as the Rockies won 16–12. Jon said, "That was a great night! How many home runs were hit?"

"Ten!" I answered.

"But Ken Griffey's was the greatest. Have you ever seen anyone hit a ball that far?"

I thought for a minute. "I don't think I've ever seen a ball hit harder than that. I'm sure that's a memory from this evening that we'll never forget."

"That, and the rain. Don't forget the rain!"

The Stadiums

As of this writing, I've seen 22 major-league stadiums. My rule is that in order for a visit to a stadium to count, I must have seen a regularly scheduled major-league game there.

These are my three favorites:

1. Polo Grounds
2. Wrigley Field
3. Camden Yards
4. Coors Field (Sorry, I can't limit it to three! And I have to include my home park.)

These are my three least favorites:

1. The Kingdome in Seattle
2. Arlington Stadium
3. Mile High Stadium (okay for football, but not baseball)

Fortunately, all three of these stadiums have been torn down and replaced by beautiful retro-parks.

Finally, I wish I could have seen games at these stadiums:

1. Ebbets Field in Brooklyn
2. Highland Park (in New York City, early in the 1900s)
3. Detroit Stadium (I planned to see it in 1982 but couldn't because of a players' strike)

TAKE ME OUT TO THE BALLPARK!

There wasn't supposed to be a ball game that night. I had checked the schedule when I'd accepted a speaking invitation several months earlier—the major-league baseball season would end the day before I arrived. Yet, there I was, driving down I-95 to Camden Yards to watch a major-league game in my twenty-second stadium.

There is a ritual I follow the first time I visit a ballpark. First, I walk the perimeter, getting a feel for the community if the location is downtown, smelling the peanuts and the sausages sizzling on the grill, listening to the vendors hawking their wares—"Hey, get your programs heeaar!"

Then, the first glimpse of a field is important. At Camden Yards, I entered along the brick warehouse that borders the concourse in right field. On my right was a wall commemorating great Orioles of the past—Brooks Robinson (the greatest third baseman of all time), Boog Powell

> *The whole history of baseball has the quality of mythology.*
>
> BERNARD MALAMUD

(a great name for a great power hitter), Frank Robinson (a triple-crown winner who led the Orioles to their first world championship), pitcher Jim Palmer (perhaps better known to younger fans for his underwear ads), feisty manager Earl Weaver, and many more.

Looking down the walkway, I noticed small baseball-sized plaques commemorating the spots where home runs had landed over the years. Along the concourse fans strolled, scanning pennants and Oriole clothing and baseball bats made to order. Then, just past the wall of fame, I had my first glimpse of the field. Rich green seats in the stands seemed to accent the deep green of the infield and outfield grass, even merging the field and the stands into one, inviting fans to not just watch but participate in the game.

Adorning the stands was the red, white, and blue bunting usually reserved for opening day, playoffs, and the World Series. This time it wasn't for the postseason, but rather was a symbol of patriotism. Plus, the home team was celebrating the career of one of its greatest players, a certain Hall of Famer. A huge banner on the facing of the press box said it all: "Thanks, Cal," it read in the black and orange of the Orioles.

Everywhere you looked, there were tributes to Cal Ripken. His uniform number—"8"—was stenciled on third base. The numeral 8 was cut into the center-field grass. And on all sides of the Legg Mason skyscraper beyond center field, the office lights were lit to form that number. As Cal played the final six games of his career, this week was simply a lovefest, and fans could remember it by purchasing commemorative programs, coffee-table books, mugs, baseballs, bobble-head dolls, hats, T-shirts, and trading cards.

This was a school night, and yet there seemed to be an inordinate number of fathers and sons at the game. There was a comfort in this ritual—just as their fathers had taken them to the ballpark, so these dads *needed* to have their sons here tonight. For a moment, I too longed to have one of my sons with me, and as I glanced at my ticket, I knew the reason why. "Originally Scheduled 9/11" it read. We fathers needed this ritual—we needed baseball—to help restore order to the world.

Cal Ripken symbolized the best that baseball has to offer. He was the kind of sports hero America loves to love. For 20 years and 2,632 consecutive games—500 more than the original iron man, Lou Gehrig—he gave his all for one team. In an age of hot-dog superstars, he quietly plied his trade, putting in hours of hard work every day, year after year. When the fans lauded him, he returned their affection, patiently signing autographs for all who wanted just a minute of his time.

Now he was facing the final six games of his career while mired in a horrendous slump. In the first inning of that evening's game, he made a throwing error. He hadn't had a hit in more than a week. Still, every time he took his turn at bat,

> *Wonderful night.*
> *Great seats.*
> *Sing the song.*
> *Have a dog.*
>
> KEITH HERNANDEZ
> *Pure Baseball*

the crowd rose as one to pay tribute and remained standing for the entire at-bat. When he feebly struck out or popped to short, the crowd would groan, then applaud appreciatively and sit down.

The game was a classic pitching duel, and the crowd sat subdued, absorbing the tense drama. The biggest ovation came in the third inning—for a section of Baltimore firefighters who had helped in the rescue effort at Ground Zero in New York City. In the middle of the seventh inning, the game stopped. Ballplayers removed their hats and placed them over their hearts. Fathers put their arms around their sons. And everyone sang "God Bless America." Thirty thousand fans were praying as one for the nation.

Going into the bottom of the ninth, I felt confident about the ending to this evening's drama. The score was 1–0 in favor of the Toronto Blue Jays, who had their closer on the mound. But Cal was batting second, so obviously, as so often before in his career, he was destined to be the hero. I envisioned a home run to tie or win the game.

Unfortunately, life often interferes with our dreams. Tonight, with all of us on our feet, collectively willing a base hit, quality pitching overpowered an aging hitter who'd lost a little of his great reflexes. A called third strike sent him

back to the dugout, and a moment later, Toronto walked off the field victorious.

I could not stay away from Camden Yards. Two nights later, I was back in the ballpark to witness an intergenerational drama. During my first visit to the park, in the top of the ninth inning Tim Raines Jr. had made his major-league debut. As a defensive replacement in center field, he made a nice catch at the wall. The next day the Baltimore management acquired Tim Raines Sr., and he was in uniform for the final game of the Toronto–Baltimore series.

Again, fathers and sons seemed to predominate in the crowd, and I could imagine each of them thinking of what it would be like if they were playing together on this field of dreams. What man wouldn't want to play in the majors with his boy? On that night, the younger Raines showed the foreshadowings of a long and productive career, scoring three times. The perfect climax to this story should have come in the seventh inning, when the elder Raines came to bat as a pinch hitter, with a chance to drive his son home from second base. This marked only the second time in major-league history that a father and son had played together in the same game.

But again, real life could not match fiction. Tim Sr. lined to right for an out, and the chance for an emotional high point passed.

The crowd continued to rise and honor Number 8, but his career was ending with a fizzle. As the O's lost 7–6, Ripken's career-worst slump was extended to zero hits in his last 32 at-bats.

So my pilgrimages to Camden Yards ended without the memorable climax I had longed for. Still, I felt satisfied.

So what if Tim Raines Sr. hadn't driven home his son—at least they had played together.

Sure, it was sad that Cal Ripken hadn't been able to break out of his slump, but that in no way diminished his great career.

And I, a father with two sons, was there to savor those dramas. Two more ballpark memories were built, ones I could share with my boys.

Those two nights reminded me again that this magnificent sport has handed down to fathers and sons a priceless ritual that gives order to their world—and, I hope, will continue to do so for generations to come.

Baseball and Space Travel

My memory of one of the greatest events of the twentieth century is linked to a baseball game.

The hardest part of our family's move west from New York City in 1964 was losing the daily broadcasts of major-league baseball. After five years of drought, the Pacific Northwest finally got its own major-league team, and I was able to follow the Seattle Pilots via radio.

On July 19, 1969, I listened as the Minnesota Twins jumped out to a six-run lead, only to have the Pilots come back and tie the game with three runs in the bottom of the ninth.

As the teams entered extra innings, a news bulletin interrupted the broadcast to announce that the Apollo 11 capsule had entered into orbit around the moon. While three men, 250,000 miles from home, prepared to descend to the lunar surface, the Twins and Pilots played on, inning after inning. Finally, at 1 A.M., they were stopped by curfew.

The game resumed the next afternoon, only to be stopped again while the fans attending listened as the lunar module descended to Tranquility Base. All of us held our breath until we heard Neil Armstrong utter these words: "The Eagle has landed." Then, as the astronauts rested on the moon, the Twins scored four times in the top of the eighteenth inning to win the longest game I've ever watched or heard as a fan.

That night, Neil Armstrong took man's first steps on the moon.

Isn't that the dream of many boys—to travel in space, and to play major-league baseball? I did both in my imagination on that July day more than 30 years ago.

A Few Reasons I Love Baseball

I LOVE BASEBALL FOR THE SOUNDS…

…of a wood bat connecting solidly with a ball
…of a fastball smacking into the catcher's mitt
…of a vendor yelling, "Hey, get your hot
dogs heeaar!"
…of a kid crushing empty soda cups with his heel just to hear the sound echo
in the concourse

I LOVE BASEBALL BECAUSE…

…I might see a no-hitter today
…"It's going, going, gone!"
…"Can you believe that great fielding play!"
…a game is never over till it's over

I LOVE BASEBALL BECAUSE IT'S FUN TO DISCUSS…

…was the runner safe or out?
…when is it time to relieve the starting pitcher?
…are the fielders positioned correctly?
…do you start the runner to stay out of the double play?

AND FINALLY, I LOVE BASEBALL BECAUSE NO MATTER HOW POORLY MY TEAM IS
PLAYING THIS YEAR…

…they can still win tonight!